Cover & Illustration by: Briana Yarrington

ISBN: 979-8-9988355-2-0

Printed in the United States of America.

No Coward Soul Is Mine
By Emily Brontë

No coward soul is mine
No trembler in the world's storm-troubled sphere
I see Heaven's glories shine
And Faith shines equal arming me from Fear

O God within my breast
Almighty ever-present Deity
Life, that in me hast rest,
As I Undying Life, have power in Thee

Vain are the thousand creeds
That move men's hearts, unutterably vain,
Worthless as withered weeds
Or idlest froth amid the boundless main

To waken doubt in one
Holding so fast by thy infinity,
So surely anchored on
The steadfast rock of Immortality.

With wide-embracing love
Thy spirit animates eternal years
Pervades and broods above,
Changes, sustains, dissolves, creates and rears

Though earth and moon were gone
And suns and universes ceased to be

And Thou wert left alone
Every Existence would exist in thee

There is not room for Death
Nor atom that his might could render void
Since thou art Being and Breath
And what thou art may never be destroyed.

Introduction

This book began in the unpolished margins of life. In pursuit of the "reasonable" and "heedful" boxes we are conditioned to check off, my passion—writing—took a backseat for years. This book began in Notes apps and voice memos. It began with FaceTime calls to friends saying, *"Hey, I wrote a poem, wanna hear it?"* In folding laundry and lunch breaks. It bloomed in the quiet moments no one saw.

Life expected so much from me:
"Be good."
"Start thinking about settling down."
"Be a dependable employee."

The list could go on…

But something in me said no—

and it only grew louder each time it was hushed.
That *something* brought these pages to your hands today.

You Are Loved (Just the Same) is not a resolution.
It asks more than it answers, and therefore, is not here to offer lessons wrapped in bows. This self-published rebellion came from hands that have shaken in adrenaline's wake, calloused under pressure, and held the wrong lovers' hands. It came from a body that endured.

This is a reflection of inventing someone you haven't met yet— a witness to your becoming.
In these pages, you'll pull back curtains and open tents. You'll finally look under the bed with the lights off. And

a flashlight will appear—with possibilities that arrive because we dared look for them.
I hope the pages in this bind illuminate a willingness to dismantle anything attempting to dim you. I hope it helps you see yourself through an honest, expansive lens.

And when you do,
I hope you like what you find.
I hope this journey leaves you certain of nothing but one thing:
You are loved. Just the same.

A Father— Anything

A father will do anything for his child.
Like get a pickup truck
To haul horses he didn't want.

When the day comes for you to learn to drive,
A father hands you the keys and says,
"If you can drive this, you can drive anything"

A father demands respect in exchange for his protection,
and really, it is a reasonable price to pay.
For such a great gift. Because:

A father will make you laugh,
hysterically so,
When you thought you forgot how to smile.
A father will make you forget
What you were sad about in the first place.

A father will make recipes,
then forget to tell anyone where they are before dying.
An invisible sign on the surgery door that says
NO SWEET POTATO RECIPES BEYOND THIS
POINT.

A father will do anything for his child
Like leave this life early to teach you
"If you can survive this, you can survive anything."

Book of Genesis

On the day the world was born—
As it so often is—
It was the day God said:
Begin. Again.
As He so often does.

Beware the Woman

Beware the woman who works in the shadows.
All her pain, flaws, and blood—she has made hallowed.
She'll smile by day, heard what you *meant* to say—
Watched gospel take mold from ego's clay.
(*See womb-envy 5:22.*)
Once, she shrank to fit the mold,
Let hands hack her small enough to hold.
When devotion spelled surrender,
and thought someone would take care of her
Until love became a noose she tied around herself.
Where agreement meant surrender, and
silence spelled survival—

But no more.
Now the woman works with the mirrors,
Who forges life new and melts steel-beam illusions,
Now, betrayal is scripture—
and the words write themselves.
Visions your eyes would rather crack than see
For every time she had to turn a blind one
Beware the woman who's learned the art of release,
Who knows when glass shatters in your palms,
how soft it can be.

She meditates by the river that feels like home,
Unlocking her mind—the only true tome.
Dolphins appear the very next day,
An unlikely omen, less likely to stay.
And perhaps it'd be cliché to say—
If you torch her, she'll befriend the flames.
But to put it simply,
And perhaps more clearly:

You are base metal.
She is gold.
She will alchemize
every stone you throw.

Lot's Wife

Do not fear burning bridges
of cities you've outgrown.

When you could just as readily
pack up
and build your own.
When angels, cloaked as hunches,
knock against your chest,
remember: angels do not fold their wings.
They widen
and they push.

The road behind?
No longer yours.
Forget the path.
Forget the stone.
They'll tell you safety's a lifeline—
its walls will keep you whole.
But what is life
if not the leaving?
The breath
without the soul.

Lot's wife was punished
not for longing.
Nor struck by simple grief.
It was the weight of hesitation
that turned her bones to grief.

A city does not keep you captive,
a paycheck,
nor a name.

But a heart that beats
in backward motion—
will kill you
all the same.
The ones before you
built with caution.
Steady hands.
Without question.
Do not freeze
at the threshold,
waiting for a better day—
a smoother road,
a brighter sign,
an omen
you should stay.

Step forward.
Doubt will follow.
Give it a seat at the table
Let it cough up smoke.

What's burning
is already gone.

It's not enough
to walk away.
You mustn't leave the front door cracked.
Come!
Let's go—
And never look back.

Mortal Sin

I say this without exaggeration.
I say it sans apology.
It is a sin
to see someone worthy,
capable of so much—
and allow them
to settle for less anyway.

A Seussian Rejection of Corporate Culture

I do not like these jobs, you see—
A corporate life is not for me.
They dress it up in suits and ties,
But underneath? A heap of lies.

A job, they say, will make you proud!
But not if you are lost in crowd.
A cog, a click, a smiling face—
Just to help the clocks keep pace.

They want your soul from eight to six,
And on the route—two-hour trips!
They'll build towers in cities bright
Then say, "Go live somewhere cheaper—right?"

They'll smile and nod, then underpay—
then be surprised when you can't stay.
They preach of "growth" and "equity,"
But hoard the gold and trickle pee.

Coffee brews decadently,
Where screens hum hot and souls turn cold.
No joy ignites— no fire glows.
Just dreary radiation light.

You'll get a badge, a cube, a screen.
An anthem of the same routines.
They'll offer "meals." But served with grins—
Soviet breadlines are still a sin.

Trays of gray, and beige buffets—
Served up in cost-cutting ways.
You dare complain? "Ungrateful!" Shouts
"You should be thrilled! Don't you dare pout!"

And dress codes! Oh, the rules you'll see—
No words! No flair! And certainly
No open shoes or shoulders bare.
But to ask *why*, you wouldn't dare.

Moral codes are worse by far—
They like us bland, prefer us par.
Don't think aloud, don't dare dream big—
Or wonder if the ladder's rigged.

You'll learn to smile through every slight.
And RSVP to "Fun Thursday Nights!"
With seed oil snacks and off-brand beer—
And Accounting whispers in your ear.

They'll drain your calendar, weeks and youth—
But worst of all yet? They'll shush your truth.
Your fire, voice, your spark, your soul—
They'll bind it snug on payroll goals.

But some hearts do remember still,
What life was like with *want* and *will*.
And they refuse to play pretend—
So, I declare: this is the end!

I do not like this culty-catch.
This gray box life, with badge and traps.
I will not sell my dreams to suits.
I will not yearn of fake pursuits.

I do not like it—can't you see?
It was not built for those like me.
And so, I skip. I hop. I run.
To build a life beneath the sun.

Cover Letter

Lauren Kalli
Cloud 9th Realm of The Souls Unbothered
Somewhere Between 444 and 1111
lauren@kalli.verse.hvn | (123) 456-7890
March 31, 2025

Hiring Manager
Caging Earth Angels LLC
666 Abyss of Dead Dreams Lane
Doomtown, Corporate Hell Hall 00000

Dear Hiring Manager (or whoever signed the blood contract to be you),

I am writing despite having no interest in your position at (insert boring company here), as advertised on (whatever soul-draining website I found you on). With an unfortunately high number of years of experience in (boring industry or role), I am confident in my ability to contribute meaningfully to your team and support your company's goals—before growing tired of forcing interest and disappearing without a moment's notice.

In my previous role at (other soul-dimming firm), I successfully ruffled lots of feathers, resulting in a questionable industry reputation. I am not proficient in Excel, nor will I pretend to be. I am particularly skilled in the art of defiance, skepticism, and meditation. I take pride in my ability to pivot career paths with religious-like fervor. Given the opportunity, I will do this at your firm at some point before the two-year mark.

I am passionate about quantum physics, portals of healing, and thought transmission. I am excited for the opportunity to bring discord, mischief, and sparkling clouds of unicorn dust-fueled rebellion to (Caging Earth Angels LLC).

Should you wish to proceed with this cosmic mismatch, I would be open to further discussing how my background, skills, and ethereal aura may rearrange your team's goals. Thank you for your consideration, time, and inevitable confusion.

With low-key love and high-key menace,

Lauren Kalli

The Compass

"What about your bills?!"
"What if it all fails?!"

Come, despite my not inquiring
in sailing lessons
from people
who are wading the shore.

The warning cries to stay the same
come from people
I wouldn't trade places with.

You can love people
And detect their error
In the same breath.

You can love people,
Hear their concern,
Then send it out to sea.

The wails of:
"How unreasonable!"
"How reckless!"

Come from people
who croak like marionettes
under puppeteers
they've never met.

And you think you should listen to them?

Why should anyone listen to them when
there's an ever-calibrating compass
pointing you in the direction
the fearful don't look.

Put down their map,
to find true north.

Disney World

Heroin addicts work at Disney World.
Unfaithful men, the corporate world.
One's hooked on needles,
the other hooked on skirts.

Meeting you was like a magic carpet ride.
That wasn't worth anyone's time.

I'd heard stories, captain Rick,
you and your un-jolly Roger.
The flags that get raised—
the planks that get walked.

No mentor came with me.
Just faith trust and pixie dust.

Met with unwanted comments jokes and leers.
I'm just a Cinderella in this boy world after all.
Out here sweeping, making livings.
Bold of you to assume
I'd sweep under your misgivings.

I had to search through hallways—
lurk around corners and knock on doors,
as if for some secret attraction,
The Hunchback of *'What is this fucking game anyway?'*

Your energy thick as a July afternoon.
The straw you imagine me sucking
Brought up once it isn't too soon.
Sweat beads dripping like scripts unspoken.

"Be warm, be friendly, but don't give it all away."
Suddenly you realize this is all a mistake.

After a half hour of Gaston-level gloating
I finally asked the Chesire rat:
What would it take to earn your business?
A phrase in sales training
We are encouraged to ask.
"I value hard work,"
you said like a riddle.
I leaned in for the pause—
(But only a little)

I said 'What does that look like
If you don't mind my asking?'
"You know"
(No, I really don't)
"Just getting to know each other better
Spending time and hanging out."

You're no Medusa
but I turned still as stone.
Till I heard the way finders say,
'Child. You are not alone.'

I'm smaller in stature,
degrees and network.
But words are my weapons
hook line and sunk.

"At what capacity?" I ask
with daring blue corn moons in my eyes;

"And at what frequency?"
Clasping my hands.

You answered as expected,
But gave it some thought
"Maybe start with dinner?"
How quaint a thought.
How charming, how grand!
Would a male sales rep,
get the same offer in hand.

I say your wife's name
Who I researched before.
"Will she be joining dinner,
or would she think it a chore?"

"It's time for you to go."
Captain Rick said!

"Me you, your wife,
It's a good idea! No?"

You shake your head
and start pacing around
"Well, you're awfully quiet."
I say.
"Sit down. I want more."

When I refused to get up
Yawned and checked my claws.
You looked like a kicked muskrat

"Any fun plans this summer?"

My smile grew wide.
"Just Disney World this year."
And I lit up like a magic castle.

"Enjoy the rides" I said.
"And don't step on a needle!"
Sharp edges are everywhere—
even if you don't see them.

The Bear

One thousand pounds—
of pure primal muscle.
Prey-drive, hungry—
with incisor teeth.
And still, somehow—
Bear
is what so many chose.

There is a poem somewhere I can't publish

because of a document I signed.
But if you listen carefully —
it whispers through the bind.

What Do Women Want
After Kim Addonizio

I want a big dog.
I want him badly behaved!
I want him calf-skin collared and
people to avoid us like the plague.
I want him ruthless and in-tact!
This dog, so no one has to guess
what's underneath. I want to walk down
any part of the world and feel safe
with all those teeth he loves to show.
Right past Tiffany's velvet ropes,
The gas station, DMV,
past the construction workers
whose cat calls will turn to kitty cries
From the sheer bass of my dog's stride.
I want to walk like I'm the safest
woman on earth and I can go anywhere.
I want that pup bad.
I want his bite history
to confirm your worst fears about dogs,
to show you how little he cares for you
or anything except me.
When I find him, I'll bring him home
from the shelter like choosing a sword
to guard me against this world,
through the wolf-cries and the snarl-mouths—
we'll go everywhere like warnings.
It'll be the goddamned
dog they bury me with.

The Wait Is Over

The wait is over.
The book is closed.
The six is wands.
The sky has opened.
The battle's won.
The fate is sealed.
The deal is done.

The wait is over,
Thank God, finally.
The wait is over,
Thank God,
Finally.

American Woman

Everyone wants to be an American woman.
Even the American men.

They want to be
spoiled,
smooth-palmed,
reality-tv stuffed,
daddy'd by someone
with two **XX** chromosomes
and a platinum Amex.

They pout through pursed lips and
post selfies from the driver's seat
of cars their parents bought.

Cry when you don't mother them,
and moan when you do.

They scroll through photos all day
of women they wish
they could possess
half the magic of.

They want to be
looked up to,
bowed down to.
They want to suck dry
your backbone
and faith in humanity.

Everyone wants to be an American woman, right?
Not the Himba women of Namibia,
who build the homes and keep the men outside them.

Nor the Mosuo matriarchs of China,
who pick lovers like produce
and kick them out before the dawn.

Everyone wants to be an American woman, you see?
Not the Umoja women of Kenya.
who outlawed men like the poison
they so often prove to be.

But here, in the land of lip filler
and girl-boss-eras,
our men want to be us—
Pursued, chosen,
protected, and cherished.
Held when they cry,
which they so often do.

The perfect combination of sexy and cute.

I'm not afraid to admit, the American women
don't hold a candle to the
nomadic nocturnal skin of the Himba
or the autonomous afterglow of the Mosu
or the bargain-less boundaries of the Umoja.

I have greater dreams in mind
than being an American woman.

I can admit this,
'cause I am not an American man.

I Knew a Girl

An obituary for the path not taken

With galaxies inside her bones.
Her boyfriend used to message other girls—
then she had his kid.

She used to go outside.
Used to laugh and
she was something wild.

There are multitudes of
what she *could've* been.
This is not even to say
it's what she *should've* been.

But, she said she wanted to travel—
That humans were meant to see the world.
But instead of that she settled
For a small apartment of a life.

Instead of following the magic,
She's just somebody's wife.
When people don't follow their dreams—
it haunts me late at night.

Courage

It took courage
for Evelyn to tell the executives at her company
the script rewrites were
from a powerful man in New York.
All the while—
She was the powerful man in New York.
Look up the origins of the word 'cunning.'
You'll see me smiling— cause the executives
they praised him, preened for him,
they all but pre-came for him.
Crowning genius titles to a make-believe fellow.
Circle jerked for fiction's phantom—
unseen and unnamed.
Their guru was a 28-year-old girl,
on the couch with her hypoallergenic dog,
and a fresh manicure.
The laptop burning on her thighs, even
seasoned sailors would leap for—and die.
Just mere weeks before there was "no room in the
budget," not even a penny to spare for her raise.
But offered thousands upon thousands
For a contract with the lingerie-wearing
Wizard of 5th Ave.
"Just tell us what he wants!" they said.
Knowing Evelyn,
It took grace not to humiliate them—
as I certainly would have.
To reveal the masculine mogul
they worshipped
was a woman's wit deferred.

It'll take courage when she lifts the veil—
and sees them go off the rails.
"Liar-ess!" "Witch!"—
are some things they might call her,
If they're having a good day—
instead of admitting wrong.
That would take courage.
A trait for which they long.

It took courage for Christie,
the independent proprietor,
to close her business doors.
To trade high-level consults for rock-a-bye babies.
To trade spreadsheets for diaper bags.
Business checkings for finger paint sessions.
It took courage to tell her clients
She's following a different course.
She is now a full-time mom.
And does not need your appeal.
No Instagram reel, no applause to be heard—
just the quiet conviction and
Just the glow of love flows to
for the few who have courage.
"What about your independence, Christie?"
"Don't you care about your dreams?"
But holy became bedtime stories,
and Christmas PJ shopping.
She chose to raise the next heroes of America
With equal parts sugar and steel—
And that, my friend
is a really goddamned big deal.
She gave her soul to something true,
Which people now so rarely do.
She showed courage in a world
That as we know— so scarcely does.

It took courage for me
to leap away from a job
with only a subscription to a writing system
a step below Microsoft Word—
and some shit to say.
It took a hit of insanity to say—
"Be gone these benefits! This 401k!
I don't want this pension."
Can't visit Versailles on company culture.
or spread wings on monthly team calls.
Everyone said,
"You're being unreasonable, Lauren!"
"You're being reckless."
But the divine tyrant was steadier
in the declaring: "This is not enough."
And hasn't steered wrong once.
So I took the fool's journey,
jumped without looking—
With no parachutes in sight, no double-checking.

I'd rather choose one second of Evelyn,
one ounce of Christie—
a pinch of my audacity.
I'd rather choose courage.

The bravest thing you can do
is believe that the net will appear
simply because you will it to.
as voices scream "Don't jump!"

It takes courage
Because it's what you're supposed to do.

Stormborn

(Inspired by Game Of Thrones)

All men must die—
but it didn't have to be this way.

I have my ideas of justice—
and the dragons have theirs.
Lately, they've been flying low.

they don't negotiate with cowards
or parlay with the fools.

The dragons' ideas of justice
Are worse than all your fears.

I wish I could protect
Everyone who's wronged me—
I do.

'Cause last night I heard them saying:

*The next time they raise their voice at her will be the last time they
have a larynx.*

*They say the kingdom's cracking
they think she's gone insane
because she smelled the smoke
before they saw the flame.*

The dragons smell when justice bleeds
and revenge,

they reap and reap.

I guess the difference
between the dragons and me
is they see more than I see.

All men must die— yes
but it didn't have to be screaming.

I wish I could've saved them
from screaming as they died.

The dragons' ideas of justice
are even worse than mine.

Full Fat Milk

Oh,
Did they try to skim you into something thinner?
something easier, something lighter
'Told you people would like you more?
If you were like almond water,
smoother and sweeter?
Content being the afterthought
in some vegan's cup?

Oh,
They asked 'have you tried oat milk?'
that slick wet velvet on the tongue,
It's in fashion.
It's safe and sweet.
Just like you
ought to be.

You almost can't tell the difference
until hunger comes the next minute.

You were never meant to decide
between mediocre alternatives to fullness.
You have history. You are *full-fat*.
Bold on the lips and hard on the gut.

With presence born from thundering herds
of prized Jersey cattle

Let the lactose-incapable
reach for something milder
Something that doesn't come

From the beating heart of beasts.

Do not be reduced
by a single molecule
to spin up a version
That offends no one

You are full fat milk.
thick with valor,
steeped in truth.

too great a beast
to land safe
in every mouth.

Gift of the Magi

There is an old Christmas tale,
published 1905,
By a man who witnessed love
And called it irony.

Someone Borrowed

I met you on a train platform—
with my feet on the concrete
and the snow starting to fall.

The EMS said that it was
"Disgusting actually."
But you didn't seem to mind.
You never seemed to mind.

I couldn't let you go or off my mind.
I hunted you down and found you
like an episode of Criminal Minds.

I wasn't looking for you when we met
But that train platform was built for us.
The eye contact we made
A silent contract you might stay.

After many nights without a plan
You brought red wine to my roof top.
Then you peed on our walk
Like you meant to mark the block.

I loved you without varnish.
Like a girl loves her dog—
knowing there will always be
something wild inside it.
And will never say it back.

My whole life has been poetry.

And you are no exception.
My whole life, a story—
With love interests too big
to sustain on this planet.

You looked at me
with a hunger you'd spent a lifetime quelling.
Like you'd waited eons
for me to make you feel brand new.
And then—
you asked me to go away with you.
But after all that waiting—
of the laborious kind—
we never stretched those country roads.
It wouldn't fit the rhyme.

In fact—
You never even followed up.

I was small next to you
With big things rushing through my mind.
Like how we're blueprints for twin-flames
Turns out you burn fast—
and I— un-contained.

So I'll tell the old story
that so few will believe
about how we lived, loved and married
before 1 AM.

Turns out the magic that's inside of me—
A wish that wriggled free—
Was only ours to borrow.

Never ours to keep.
Like the card game on the mattress—
The one that we both won—
like your hands were made for poker,
and mine were made for fun—
The kind that always ends
with the rising of the sun.

And when they fell asleep
It was holding each other.

My hands were made for feeding you
when you'd bite me anyway.
They knew the silence to follow
Nevertheless, they packed the suitcase
wishing fate away.

But there's magic that's inside you
that wasn't mine to keep.
That has not once stopped me—
From packing anyway.

Want

I don't want to know what cologne you're wearing—
though it smells delicious.

Don't care how many girls came before me.
Just tell me the secret ingredient
in your grandma's recipe.

I don't want to know the rent on this place,
or how many have stayed the night before.

Don't want to know
if you find someone prettier,
or if there's someone else you're talking to.

I simply… don't want to know.

I want to know how you ended up here.
Why you stayed.

I want to know
why New York is so cold this time of year—
and why, when it snows,
it's only briefly beautiful.

I'd like to know what the engine's heat feels like
on a ferry ride through a blizzard to see you.

I want to know
what ran through your mind
the night your brother died.

It's killing me.

I have to know:
do you really think
it was his time to go?

It's so easy.
Just tell me what I want to know.

Hoboken

In my younger and more vulnerable years,
I too may have settled for Hoboken—
keeping skylines and rental rates at bay.
Manhattan, safe body of water away

Then I would have thrown parties,
Hoping someone from ~~West Egg~~,
I mean New York
Would stumble in one night
And say I'm certainly glad to see you again.

You love the city, but you wouldn't get a keychain for it,
Quiet eye contact that gut-throat-screams about what
could have been
They're a rotten crowd, Hoboken!
You're worth the whole damn bunch put together!

I know I smashed things up,
then retreated back
into my money and let other people
worsen the mess I made.

Just know I think of you often.
And if I'm your past—
I hope one day
you beat against the current
back to me.

The Helen Complex

Don't be that guy.

You know the one.
The *"the thing is"* guy.
No one likes a *"the thing is"* guy.

Even less the *"it's not the right time"* guy,
or the *"the distance is too much"* guy,
and least likable of all—
the *"I love you, but"* guy.

Oof.

No one likes those guys.
I don't know why they keep making them.
Truly,
the demand doth not warrant the supply.

Halt the horses of the assembly line!
Try again.
Dig up the DNA from the Spartans.
And feed the Helen Complex.

Bring back sword fights,
abductionary seductions.
Summoning gods to intervene.
Bring back the golden apples—
and feed them to a Trojan horse.

Bring back Olympian level courtship!

Bring back the:
"I don't care what Menelaus' Herculean men will do."
"I don't care what they marched for."
The red cloaks are otherworldly in battle.
"But the thing is—
I don't want a world without you, Helen."

Be that guy.

The one undeterred
by Hercules
or property rights.

Bring me one with a smudged reputation!
And a kingdom-sized middle finger
of an apology for it.

Bring me the guy who knows
After the war is over—
my place is in perfumed bubble baths
in marbled palaces.

I'm bored.
Bring my Helen Complex
72 grapes.

Bring me
another Troy to burn.

Willpower and Spite

If I had a dollar
for every guy who told me
he wanted to be
a writer,
a "creative,"
an actor—

I'd have loads of money,
a lot of willpower,
and a lot of spite.

Something tugs at me,
when two men I dated—
back-to-back—
were chasing the same dream
and still managed
to carry on like clichés.

It felt coordinated.
Like they were in on some joke
and it was premeditated.

So often underestimated:
my willpower
and my spite.

It seems the whole world
runs experiments
just to see how far it runs.

While we're here—
Would you like to see?

2017 – 2023

I wonder if there will be clues—
claw marks on the casket.
I almost had you.

My fillings. My molars.
A strand of DNA.
I wonder which artifact
will give it all away,

They found me
with my hair ripped out.
"It's just a shame
he wasn't caught."

No detective found the source,
argued with their voices hoarse.
Everything was decomposed—
except the left hand,
empty— unproposed.

Told you I'd never get over you.
Did you think I was lying?
I plan to spend eternity
lying here—
trying.

They'll lay me down,
I'll find no rest.
In Times New Roman:
She Failed the Test.

I Loved You

like no one else
will love your NPD ass.
not with the grace I did,
not with the poise I did.
Hands shaking but
arms open.

My friends told me to leave but,
I
Loved
You.

They'll get your charm.
I took your poison—
that barbed wire tannin from the tongue.
Spider webs woven
So finely
I didn't know I was in them.

They might love you, sure.
But will they swallow your
unique, lethal brand of poison?
Gulp by mother-fucking gulp?
Will they call it wine?
Respond by saying *it's not your fault*
You just haven't been loved enough.

No.
No one will love you like I loved you

I held your *rage*

Like a peacefully sleeping child.
I let him *rest*.

Will you throw tantrums with others?
Like you did with me?
When you didn't like the tone I used
when I asked you
to turn the phone volume down
at 2 a.m.
on a weeknight?

Maybe you just didn't love me
The way I loved you.

The only strategy, then, was to become softer
until the storm hit center
and I had no shelter.

So I signed your demons up for kindergarten.
dressed them up to take school photos.
"Smile, Asmodeus!"
Kissed their little red foreheads,
and made chicken noodle soup
for their rotten little souls.

I lined them up on rainbow carpets.
Gave them crayons,
took their matchsticks.

When I asked the evil in you to come outside—

You made me believe
it was coming from me
this whole time.

My compassion, a velvet wrapped guillotine
where I lost my head
but kept my heart.

My giving up, a treaty signed postmortem
The shaking hands
finally fall limp

Because no one will love you like I loved you.
Not
Even
Me.

Boxer

They say he was the *strongest* one,
but strength does not mean safe.
it only means *first*—
first to lift,
last to break.

Too worn to ask why
either way.

He told me he loved my steadfast nature,
my fortitude—
my hardy stature.

Then handed me bricks for his mill
which he said was for us—
but spun only for him.

I sweat into the mortar
Like it was my fucking job
The greater the limp,
The greater reward.

He was the kind of pig
who prefers cracked hooves
over bright eyes,
grass bellies.

He was the kind of pig
who wore suits to the slaughterhouse—
Like the gatekeeper of morality

he hailed himself to be.

To every disappointment I said:
"I will work harder."

I was an enormous beast—
Eighteen hands high,
in metaphor at least.

Had the strength of *two ordinary horses'*
strength combined

But deep down I knew:
The day my coat went dull,
He'd adjust his tie
And write my name
on the side of the truck.

The day I'd hear the sound
of him being my equal—

The sound of a pig's promise—
that cost too much life
to believe in.

The sound
of brick heavy dreams
I can't carry anymore.

That awful,
awful sound,
Boxer's hooves dragging
across Glue Factory ground.

Pax Romana

It was the best of times.
It was the worst of times.
It was the age of love songs
and smeared lipstick lines—
Sometimes from laughing
other times, not.

It was the best of times
because my hands were warm
with the tea you made.

It was the worst of times
because later
you'd throw the mug in the kitchen.

It was the worst of times
because it made me sick.
It was the best of times
because you rubbed my back
on bathroom tile ticks.

It was truce season with a tender stomach!
It was our bellyache and no one else's!

An era of magic.
An age of madness.

Pax Romana baby!

You held the mighty fist of reason—
raised it for good cause.

It was the brief times
doors closed quietly
once the latch corroded
from getting slammed.

It was seductive.
It was sexy
not knowing
which emperor I'd get today

Aurelius or Brutus
Claudius or Domitian.
Domitian,—
ever heard what happened to that guy?

It was the golden age of addictions
to laurel lined apologies—
medals for every time
more men could have died.

It's said all roads lead to Rome
But the map to peace times
constantly shifts.

I witnessed the peak golden age
behind two marble eyes

Vivat Imperator!
Long live you and I—

Between you and me, Domitian,
I never felt more *alive*
Than when needing spilled
Like eyeball kerosene—
and your sweetness came
in brief, golden flickers.

Pax Romana!
Those were the days.

It was the period
of packing bags quietly—
then being coerced out of leaving.

Bring me back!

To a generation
of obsession-forged magic—
glimmering brighter
once turning tragic.

I'm bathing
in the ashes of the aqueducts,
calling it Pax-Romantic.

soy boy beta cuck

My friends and I used to call you
'*soy boy beta cuck*'
and it had nothing to do with you being a pescatarian.
That was just a happy coincidence.

We called you *'soy boy beta cuck,'*
*b*ecause you threw temper tantrums.
Inherently irrational, instinctually insane.
As if the people in your life
were on line for tickets
for a horrible one man show.

The saddest part of your... *performances,*
is you thought it was the work
of pure MacArthur genius—
Where Ben Shapiro rivals Bosch
Dennis Reynolds sketches DaVinci
Justin Timberlake's boots
on the ground at Benghazi.
You pounded your fat fists on the ground
When no one agreed with you—
And thought it righteous.

They don't give out Pulitzers
for getting angry.
Or convenient forgetting,
wishing you could act,
or always having
something negative to say.

You will go down in history!
<u>World's Greatest</u>
<u>Highly Renowned!</u>
<u>'soy boy beta cuck'</u>
A stench you can't wash off.
A title that limps after you
like a mange-riddled mule
named Baby.

My Body is My Home

When he told me how many kids he was having—
like it'd been set in stone,
like the walls inside my body
were his to bend and mold—

But my body is my home.
A home—
that was built without a nursery

He once said
my not wanting to bear children
was the most selfish thing he'd ever heard.

But I've rented space before,
and didn't like how the guests treated it

Maybe there's an issue with the pipes,
the foyer, or the well.
But that's not the reason
it's on the market still.

my body is my home.
I'm told
it's getting older by the day,
that it's losing market value—
once worth its weight in gold.

The foundation has a few cracks, sure—
isn't that what concrete's for?

Maybe it's true, the owner's selfish—
`Cause for me, carrying a child

would be like a peanut-butter crusted knife
grating a rare marble counter.

Might be selfish, but it's true—
don't you know what it does to you?

No finger paints shall be smeared
on this estate cabernet.

And do you hear that lovely sound?
No?
Oh- it's the quiet.

The blueprint is not up
for anyone's debate.
My body is my home—
leave suggestions at the gate.

No one would questions
these locks on a man's house.

They'd say,

That space is his to live in—
he owes no one guests.

This body's mine to live in
I'll wreck it if I like
This home is mine.
Keep walking—
you don't live on this block.

General Daydream Disorder

Don't know if it's the road, or the tires,
or the motion
massaging its weight
around the circumference of my skull
Maybe it's the song on the speakers,
A warm bouncy melody
made for someone,
easier than me.
Someone who can listen to the music,
look out the window,
and enjoy the ride.

But I'm halfway between wake and sleep
and the difference has never mattered less.

I blink slow—half-mast heavy lids
the trees stretching outside,
pulling the world into streaks of green.
Then—
A crack.
Branches breaking, something too fast,
too frantic, too quick to survive.
Innocent, cloven hooves
inches away
from my eyes.

eyes glossy with a terror
too ancient to name.
The car swerves.
But the deer is half in and out the windshield.

and the difference has never mattered less.

metal twists in protest
and the world turns inside out,
I would wake up at this point
if I'd been asleep to begin with.

The glass may as well be jagged.
It may as well have
stifled a doe's ribs.
She might as well be inside the car
with her head against the hump.

Burnt rubber
and something copper
might as well sting the air.

All because I wondered
how taxidermy at the tag sale
wound up there.

My Body is a Haunted House

I know I've said my body is my home
But somedays,
it feels more like a haunted house—
where people have done things
they shouldn't have.
They sat around a Ouja board,
then tried to shush the spirits.

'And like all haunted houses,
there have been disputes
about where imagination ends
and reality begins.

There are days
I, myself,
do not know the difference.

But clearly there is something in it—
From which you can run
but never hide.

There are days that beg the question:

If no one's even knocking,
why doesn't it feel safe here?

Trespassers

The cafe table marked *"Reserved."*
The velvet rope at VIP events.
A stick in the ground, holding
an *"under contract"* sign,

is a siren call—
a demand for trespassers.

It's the club titled *"Members only,"*
It's the tires peeling
into the parking space
that was waiting just for you.

Statistically,
you're most likely to be pickpocketed
beside signs warning: *"Beware of pickpockets."*
We pat our pockets,
clutch our keys,
nervous tension,
onlookers' tease.

The act of guarding— holding tight—
Makes them come
Left, down, up, right.

As if it isn't already hard enough,
to keep the things you want just for yourself.

Everyone knows.
What Trespassers love most

———

the very thing marked: *No Trespassing*

Cowboy Dan - A Confession of the County Fair

Cowboy Dan, at the cattle pen.
Brown messy hair
beneath a ball cap,
aluminum pens, ready to snap.

Cowboy Dan, traveling
show to show with his dad
Who he said was the most educated -uneducated man
He'd ever met.
Now I say that about you.

I say that about him, Juliet and Othello.
The keyed up mustang with the semper-fi chain.

I was seventeen, dying to break mine.
You were looking too hot to a girl
In a fight with her first boyfriend
Who didn't know what he had or something-

blah blah blah.

Who cares.

You were steady with the cattle.
Firm, but gentle.
You had two brown eyes
That didn't quite look the same direction
and at my mention you said,
'bull riding will do that to you.'

Back by your trailer
that smelled like saddle pads and salt,
sweaty must and summer need.

Cowboy Dan looked at me in a way no one had before
and hasn't since;
Like he knew exactly how to handle me—
A chestnut mare running through barrels.

Hey, Cowboy Dan!
Remember when we told my parents
you were five years younger than you were?
Naughty Cowboy Dan.

PBR's in country fields,
Dusty hands, and pocket knives.
Yep, that's him.
That's Cowboy Dan.

That's who I was with
when my boyfriend was trying to find me.
The one who didn't know what he had
or whatever.
He wouldn't recognize me anyway
with hay in my pockets.

With the stars above us, and friends around us
A seal blocking cell phone signal
From spoiling our midnight field.

When we'd had enough of everyone else
And not enough of each other.
We got into his pickup

The road ahead sweeping
like uncertain paths to freedom
You singing songs I don't know the name of.
You pulled me into your lap going 60 down the road.
Your hands on the wheel, either side of me.

I thought 'This is crazy!' 'This is how I die!'
I don't even really know Cowboy Dan—
The very abandon my upbringing warned me against.

Then you switched the headlights off
And without a word,
Cut the wheel into someone's cornfield
parked right there like it belonged to you
In a way no one had before
And has never since.

I said, "This is trespassing, Cowboy Dan!
What if they shoot us? Don't go there!"

I said no, but I didn't mean it.

You laughed like it was just another day on the farm.
Told me not to worry about a thing.
You kissed me enough that
Eventually I didn't.

You trespassed on someone's property
But not all the way that night, Cowboy Dan.
In fact you never did, all the way.

Restraint. That's why you impressed me.

Now, when Florida Georgia Line comes on,
I think about rolling the windows up
I think about the Scoharie county fair.
I think about how fields are grown
Not for corn, but for us.

I think about
The one who turned the headlights off
just to see me glow.

Greyfriars Bobby

It's said there was a mutt in Dust Hollow
who crossed five counties lines on instinct alone—
It's said he had a nose for finding fate
Fate once found, he never let go

He walked by dozens of people on porches
Trotted past barrels and backdoor butchers
until he found a man in a work-worn hat.
resting beside a trailer.
and curled up next to him.

Their finding each other—
proof logic wants to be denied.

Greyfriars Bobby didn't bark, didn't whimper—
Didn't need to ask why.
Just rested his chin on the man's boot,
like he'd done it a hundred times before.
Like together was somewhere
They'd been, a hundred times before.

They were buried beside each other—
Ninety-eight years in dog winters apart
So true it aches—
Love that's content to wait.

True— no fine text, no chess game— love.
Love that comes cruelly
Before you learn to sit and stay.

You thought I was out of your league
But the moment I saw you,
I knew you'd bring me to a new one—
worth bearing Scotland winters for.

I knew that being next to you
meant a wagging tail my whole life.

So I ran.

I didn't know what to do
with something that would do so much for me.

So I strayed.

'Sprinted back to Dust Hollows
where I wouldn't have to face
something that sees me for all I am.

Eleven human years later
the nose of Greyfriars Bobby
brought me back to the realm of things
that guard each other's graves.

The nose of Greyfriars Bobby
brought me to the realm
of things that sit and stay.

The Noahbook - You Would've

(Inspired by The Notebook by Nicholas Sparks)

You would've written me for 365 days
365 ways of saying "Please come back."
Built that house brick by grief-laden-brick.

Walked across those leaves of grass
And Walt Whitman wondered about me.

You would've chased me through every lifetime—
Drilled through your head, nailed by your hand
Crucified to the cause of us.
Bled perfectly good blood just to see me smile.

Yeah.

You would've laid down with me at traffic lights
and walked me home in the rain.
My ex-boyfriend barely remembered my birthday,
But you would've.

My GOD you would've.

I am an uncommon woman with uncommon thoughts. I've led an uncommon life and there will be monuments dedicated to me. My name will not be forgotten, but in one respect, I have failed as gloriously as anyone who ever failed. I pushed away the one who loved me with all his heart and soul. And now, nothing else could ever be enough.

All the things you would have done for me, if I let you.
All the things I should've.

And when my perfectly fine but just-not-you fiancé
comes knocking on the door

You'd ask me,
"Do you want me to take care of this?"

And then
you would've.

Cowboy Dan's Girlfriend

Cowboy Dan's girlfriend
is probably hot.
She probably has perfect skin
without trying

She probably owns
three pairs of jeans
and if I had to guess,
has a few years on him.

If she saw me—
she'd look me up and down
and say something like
"Honey, bless your heart."

Cowboy Dan's girlfriend
likes my long blonde hair—
she imagines it slipping
down down down
creek water.

I don't want to be
unforgettable anymore.

Cowboy Dan's girlfriend
probably gains and loses
the same fifteen pounds all year.

He's too straight to notice.

She gets drunk at the bar
and flirts with his friends,

but Cowboy Dan's packin'—
Cowboy Dan doesn't care.

She probably
has one of those southern names—
a double-syllable first
and a single-syllable middle.

Stop.

I don't want to think about that.
She can't be real.
I prefer to think she doesn't exist at all.

I like to think he is sitting by
the cow-hair-crusted landline,
waiting for my call.

I like to think
she doesn't exist at all.

Honeycomb

My hand on his bare chest.
His, holding it there.
A flesh colored anchor
gone warm to hot

The way you hold something
you mean to keep—
the way you stick to it
once you do.

If You Die First

I will speak to no one
and eat nothing
for two whole days.
I will drink lukewarm coffee
from your chipped Christmas mug,
pace the gravel driveway
barefoot, so my soles remember
their direction—

In case my soul forgets
to remember you.

I'll read every receipt
ever left in your truck—
Big Macs and Agway feed.
Oil changes and
unleaded premium.
On day three,
the sun will come out
like it always does.
The sun will come out
to bestow her rich ideas upon the soil.

Everyone will help me plan your funeral.
While I sit on the Chesterfield couch
likely chosen
with customer comfort in mind.

But it's too soft for my frail bones.
My porotic ghost nearly sliding off.
Funeral Homes are not good

at the death business.
They build homes for unalive people.

A fake cactus frowns
beside plastic font options
"This one is quite elegant…
but this is our most popular."

But I wasn't paying attention.
I was trying to see
if this is real mahogany.

The grief choreographer
is going over prayer choices
And live music options.

"A harp could be quite nice!"
"Has a heavenly quality to it!"

Lord take me now.

I look down at my feet—
orthopedic heels and pantyhose,
when I'm called back to the room
with the clearing of a throat.

The idea takes root in this sunless place,
to ask for time alone.
To review the fonts.
To see what calls.

And when they leave I'll
rise from my sandy joints
And head to a folder stuffed, finger tagged

spiral bound instruction book
made just for me.
The Gravedigger's Manual.
a swell sight to see.

A book full of facts any widow
should have the decency not to know.

It can take 8–12 years for a cadaver
to decompose in pine.
Four if it's damp
and two if it's dry.
They come back in
And I let the grief choreographer
make the Moulin Rouge production
of his stage-hand dreams.

I put on my fake smile
That no one suspects is so—
Because I am an old innocent lady.

Time to pick out your suit:
It's navy and it's wool.
Something that the worms
Will have trouble chewing through.

Over the pulled pork
And trays of cornbread
from that roadside shack you loved.

I picked this meal because it's face- heavy
And will hide how much I miss you.

Photos I was too catatonic to choose from

Line the wall people point at.
"They had quite a life together."
"She's handling this all so well."

Cheese and rice.

I stay with my sister
in her tiny guest room
with coral-colored curtains
she swore she'd never get

For two whole weeks I'll lie down
might even close my eyes but—
No one will know what
I'm up to behind them.

I'm reciting the gravedigger's manual!
by candle light and cat eye glow.
Can't they see? Don't they know?

I'm memorizing how many pounds it takes
to seal a single lot.
Better hurry
it's about to snow.

One night,
I take some pills—
Not too much, just enough.
just for fun- if not the nerves.

I will expend my scarce supply
of calcium to aviary limbs
to claw my way down

and close the bird cage once more.

Like you used to close our bedroom door
Like no one has since.
and had never before.
Slow, deliberate and yearning
For no wind left behind.

Yes,

No wind left behind.

I'll take exhales that feel like climax
The release of one's rightful place.
my favorite person, his sunken face.

I'll hold your hand so tight
maggots will squirm through the seams—
washing your wedding band
wet, wild and gleaming;

Shining like it did on our wedding day
and then never did again.

Natural, we'll always be.

The thought crosses to lick one
Just to see
if they also taste like river water
and whiskey sours
like you.

Information any widow
should have the decency not to know.

I will stroke the beard
I finally let you grow out—
the one that once met my merry cheeks
and scratched them.

I will all but purr in joy.
Contentment for my rightful place.

For one last time I'll whisper:
"Goodnight baby."

For tonight if I'm mortal
and forever if I'm lucky

And to that I heard you say
Goodnight pretty baby,
I'll see you tomorrow.

A Seussian Rejection of Modern Dating

I will not text you first, dear boy,
I will not chase, I shall not ploy.
I will not plan our Saturday,
Then watch you flake and fade away.

I will not book a place to eat,
Or beg to call, 'oh how sweet!'
I will not praise your "hustle grind,"
While scrubbing dishes, moving skies

You say you want a woman soft
Yet wilt when time to take your shot
You crave devotion, fawning stares
But impact, no! You wouldn't dare!

You scroll through girls with lips so plush,
Yet fumble words and fear their touch.
Your brain is shot, attention span, too,
Sid Sweeney's rack? Too good for you!

Your jaw ever clenched, your fists grip tight,
Your ego raw, your anger ripe.
You gaslight, dodge, then whimper, whine,
and moan on and on
"The world's unfair to guys!"

I will not swipe, I will not match,
This batch's no good,
Let's start from scratch!
I do not want to "chat real quick,"
I demand a soul—
does that make you sick?

I want to know, when the plane shakes hard,
Do you take a deep breath or beg to God?

I will not sip a coffee date,
I'll take my caffeine with the greats.
I'll flirt with Frost and play with Blake
I will not sip a coffee date.

So go.
Retreat.
Cry if you must—
protect your eyes from kicked up dust.

Casual
(After 'My Man' by Chelsie Diane)

My man doesn't do casual.
Don't think he even knows the word.
He folds his socks like dead sea scrolls
and pours wine like it's blood oath.

He kisses like returning from war
after watching his buddies
get blown up.

My man is anything but casual.
He alphabetizes playlists.
and makes hypnotic eye contact
with appetizer menu options.

Oak tree stumps are his confessional
where his eyebrows ache
In the way where the tips of them
point to God and say,
"Please show me the way."

He'd drag a body if he had to
burn entire cities down
For implying I'm the problem.

He'd learn five different languages
to insult people on my behalf.
He'd buy a house on another hemisphere
and find a job there
if I wanted to visit
in the off chance I might stay.

He makes shit happen.

I'd convert religions for him in public
and he'd practice mine in secret.

This is the only way
things of worth can be done.

Uncasually—
He would smash his phone in his hands
if I took too long to reply.
He would change his entire blood type
if I happened to need type A

My man doesn't know one lick
of this 'casual,' you speak of.
My man would risk prison
if I thought raw milk would taste better
after crossing state lines.

That's the thing about him—
He's like that.
Everything on earth is like that.
all the world a course
on being un-casual.

Like the way crows build nests.
and sunflowers crane their necks.

Hurricanes do not 'casually,' flood a coast.
They make it count.
They make it show!

He treats my shadow like it has human rights.
and no one ought to step on it.
He buys my shampoo before I run out
and calls my name like gospel.

Casual?
'Never heard of her.
I don't even
know the name.

Why Is It?

When I braved the famine, brewed the venom,
Found a lovely company in the dust
that collected in the keyhole of doors
I meticulously locked
something arrives worth opening for

Why must the spring arrive the very day
My winter coat comes in, full-plumed and dark?
When every hair on my head has coarsened, bristled,
And will scar anything that brushes past it?

Why did love leave when joy met its prime?
Why did the mountain disappear-
when I grew these claws to climb?

Why does the soul bloom again
When the body begins to ache?
Too much sugar
And not enough honey

The shooting stars fly farthest
With the skylight windows closed.

Why is it- and *who* is it-
That made it like this anyway?

Psalm for Skeptics

Maybe there is no lesson.
No grand reveal. No reward.
Maybe the curtains don't rise—
because it was never a show to begin with.

Just very bright lights
on your every move.

Maybe the Dalai Lama will live to 110.
Maybe he won't.
Maybe C.S. Lewis was right to be afraid—
Not of finding there is no God,
but of finding Him cruel, indifferent.

Maybe it's okay to have trouble trusting
An all-powerful force watching children drown
In the name of contrast—
two sides of the same inflated coin.

Maybe there are no emergency exits
Because He's waiting for the water
to cover our mouths.

They say to play the cards you are dealt
and if adversity
is a winning suit,
I have a royal flush.

Whose wounds these are
I think

(maybe)
I know.

His house is subterranean though;

He will surely see me stopping here,
Where Morningstar lights
cast our every doubt

Maybe kindness and love are tactics of delay,
hiding truths lying in plain sight—
news cycles and propaganda.
Radioactive hearts gone black.

Maybe the cancer has reached the soul.

If today is any indication.
Maybe no one is coming to save.
Not family,
Not friends,
Not Cowboy Dan.

But, one thing's for certain—
refusal to consider this,
Even as a .001% possibility,
Is the mark of a small mind.
A happy one,
A simple one.
A small one.

Maybe the abyss is the only mirror—
Not in metaphor, but in mass—
Maybe the only real law

which can be relied upon
is that pressure deepens
every inch you fall.

Maybe the only matter
there is no 'maybe about'
is there's no hand to catch you
when you do.

I don't know much
about moons,
or yew trees.

But it's a quiet day
in Gethsemane.

The Travelers

They arrive at my doorstep—
wet foot and weary.
Then they tell me their names.

I feed them—
they're hungry.

Some withdraw to vacant spaces of my mind—
soft-bellied things with razor-sharp teeth,
heedless and reckless
of decorum's upkeep.

I awake to the flying around
of fairy tale birds,
waiting for my hands
To stop wiping sap from my eyes—
So they can climb aboard.

They're not long for manners.
And are known for not knocking.

Poems:
inconveniently timed
storms of regret—
rousing in the distance
in lightning neglect.

I've seen them with stubble.
I've seen them with crutches.
Blades lodged in throats.

Inside a house—
with the shutters on fire.

Stuck gazing at mirrors,
asking what others might think.
Sometimes, they echo the same sentence
over and over.
Other times, a singular white-lipped word
slips through the foggy signal
into my hand.

Some poems do not speak at all.
They just sit—
on the edge of the bed,
swinging their legs,
looking out the window—
unaware you can see them.

They come to me starving—
not for rhymes,
but for witness.
A warm, knowing look—
that knows the defeat
of one who's pounded on doors
with hearts in one's fists,
only to be turned away.

So they travel.
Town to town—
poet to poet,
in dust and pollen,
the ghosts are still hoping
to be remembered.

They want to be remembered

without saying where they've been.

The travelers step onto the carpet,
Barefoot, breathing hard,
asking if I have
a spare room,
a pen,
a heart that's brave.
And I don't have the heart
to send them away.
I have a policy for them.
And it's open door.
However, they arrive—
I don't let them wait.

Hitched

I got hitched!

I don't know if you hitched onto me,
or I hitched onto you,
or if some hand placed us together
in knots that know no unravel.

What I know is this—
books are my matrimony,
stories are my groom,
the only thing that's longed to see me
down a long cathedral isle.

In some distant past,
my name's signed in parchment!
I took this dream to have and to hold—
For richer, for poorer,
In sickness and in health.

We quarrel, we fight.
We kiss and make up.
We're just like any couple—

I vow to you, beloved:
fear will not do us part.

Even if I wanted to leave—
the alimony would be too steep.
The price of truth deferred
Is more than I can afford.

So I stay.

hitched to the craft,
bound to calling—
the amazement.
to The Travelers

To you.

The Invisible Hand

The invisible hand, Smith said,
guides us— and greed's our thread
that stitches together the common good.

The invisible hand is missing a thumb—
Maybe it's been cut off clean.

Blisters ooze on nurse's night heels.
Angry rings of sweat are drawn
on orange worksite hats.

Then of course, there are poets who leak,
who siphon pain and pour it as ink—

Nociceptor tales sold by the pound.
Tales of bed-rot from what we lay down
But we refuse to let it die— don't we?

Doctors diagnose.
The tech bros,
well… who knows—

Who knows
but only an artist
prints the fungus
beneath the cuticle

The invisible hand guides us, sure.
But art is the artery—

No limb moves without it.

And I hate to see the market bid
on tears I didn't want to give—
The wealth of nation rises
with the printing cost per stanza

"Every individual," Smith said,
"intends only his own gain"—

So I weigh each syllable
like a merchant at the dock
wishing for a utopia untouched—
That'll work in theory
but not in practice.

Maybe the tech bros are working on it.
A world—
Where musicians can sing
not for supper
but for the taste of new air.

I wish for a world
where poets may live—
not making livings on death

85 Years of Age

When I am 85 Years of Age, all those men will be right— the ones who asked girls on coffee dates and dinners at The Smith. I will have died without any children of my own next to me. There were no children of my own to depend on when I began to decline. Who will care for me then? I used to think. And then I thought… "Will I even care then?" Because when I'm 85 Years of Age my hair will be tangled with knots that even their most devout daughter couldn't brush out. My hair will have accrued these knots from spending hours racking through it for the perfect words to put into my books, for the readers I want to pass love to like a legacy. For the wonderfully meticulously and fearsomely crafted reputation I will leave behind.

When I know the time is coming, I will take my most timid student into my closet. I will let her pick her favorite outfit, …anything she likes (yes, even that). "I used to be beautiful like you a long time ago." (I have to say things like this, I'm obligated to.) She'll tell me I still am now— We'll smile because we know it's not the same and there's nothing either of us can, nor should, do about it.

She doesn't know yet the whole estate is being left to her. Her parents love her, they just weren't expecting to have a lightning streak of a child. They are a touch afraid of her power; perhaps rightfully so. It's okay because I'm not. I'm 85 years of age— and I have seen some shit. I'll make sure she takes 'the shoes.' The lucky ones. I will have my assistant throw out any of the unlucky ones beforehand so they are not kept for sentimental value. I will leave my life and my legacy and moth balls and rubies to her. She didn't know it, but I

94

did on our first lesson. All of this will be hers some day. Some day before she is 85 Years of Age- when she can enjoy it.

This girl will saddle up my horse, the one the doctors say I'm too old to ride. And watch me canter the fields. She'll laugh and cry in acknowledgment that this is real and this is joy and this is fleeting. Even my horse who pins her ears at everyone will miss my madness when I'm gone. I bought this horse 11 years ago because I liked the look in her eye. She was diagnosed with progressive navicular disease and everyone was convinced she'd be crippled in two years. Personally, I think she was faking it to find her way to me. Nature finds a way. My student will see me a bit too winded after I get off. She'll try to hide looks of well-meaning concern out of politeness. I just smile at her, my face purple as a plum. She doesn't realize— it's her turn next. I will look back in love, defiance, and awe at a life well lived, at 85 Years of Age.

On the last night, I'll show her all the poems I didn't publish. We'll laugh at how BAD they are. I playfully insult her (I'm old. I have to.) When I tear up she knows better than to point this out. We'll drink a final glass of white wine together. The wine I used to prefer red before I was 85 Years of Age and red gave me rosacea.

The death riddles will start. She'll ignore most of them but look up from her book at me towards the fireplace when it seems to really be happening. It will be calm and serene. Nature finds a way to do it this way. The stiff-boned golden retriever lays unbothered by the fireplace, his eyes in a sweet smile of sleep. He groans only briefly when I pass.

When the body stops breathing, there will be a brief moment she thinks "Fucking finally." I hope all of the energy and words that were too big to even fit through me go straight to her when I am no longer 85 Years of Age.

She takes my dog home like I told her to. That night, she whispers promises into the regal musk of his graying coat. The lawyer calls her the next day with the news. She will spend her life a chemist, mixing the intangible with permanence— and she knows exactly where she will be when she is 85 Years of Age.

Hey, God

I know we haven't talked in a while and
I don't know how to tell you this
But…
You kind of have the worst fanbase.

There I said it.

Myself included sometimes.
We're starving but we aren't hungry
For amygdala junk food.

Hey, God,
They're starting wars in your name again
Can you part a sea or something?
So we can walk through the valley together.
Why can't we stop dying
at each others hands?

And kill instead the otherness
We were sent to overcome?

Hey God—
Have you seen the news?
They've forgotten you are love again.
Can you remind them in the most amazing
And unexpected ways?
Just like you always do.

I know you can do it-
I've seen it done before.

So Hey, God —
why haven't you?

Hey God,
Your son is the coolest.
And I would've swiped right.
So thanks for letting us borrow him

A couple thousand years ago
in body or in thought—
The form matters not.

And not to be a tattle-tale, God
But Pope the Innocent
Called your daughter-in-law a whore.
and someone burned her book.

I know.
It's worse than I thought too.
Okay, I'll try to remember he's an anointed one too.

Sometimes I forget
to love as you love
God.

That the only way
is with humility
without condition

Sometimes I forget
You did not cure the blind
by yelling at them.
No.

You did it by believing
in their ability to see
When no one else did

Can you remind us,
how the words
"Peace!"
"Be still."
Calmed the sea of Galilee?
Can you give us a map to a place
Where your so called 'fanbase,' recalls
salvation without condemnation.

Hey God, can you help us out?

Christmas in April

Red and green daisies.
lilac yellow evergreens.
Wool dresses rolled up
right above the knees,

Apollo peeks through the oculus—
and reaches
for the coldest room in the house.

April doesn't suit me.
Nor does December.
Both are too dressed up.
and neither feels quite right.

Saturn, God of agriculture,
Rome would fall again,
if they saw what we did
to *Saturnalia*—
GMOs, garlands,
corn syrup loaded christmas cookies.

They used to light fires
and call chaos a holiday.

You may not like it,
You might not care,
But the word *"Easter"*
comes from *"Ostara"*—
a feast of rebirth
a festival of fertility.

Sound familiar yet?

How about
communal meals,
Eggs.
Rabbits.

Stay with me.

Seasons, like lovers,
arrive promising truth—
explicit or implied.
Expectation,
hangs like bows
a reused parade float.

If the walls of
O Little Town of Bethlehem
could talk,
they'd probably say,
they hate a world hell-bent
on lying to itself.
Where audacity like ornaments
lies sleeping in the attic—

Read the writing
on the yellow wallpaper.

Lying is killing you.

Your Easter basket
is filled with carcinogens,
and you're calling it
a feast of life?

Wheel Postulate

All science has ever been
is poetry with numbers.
Lanterns of opposites.
Bedrooms with strangers.

An amazon-spun bought—
sold for contradiction-value,
beacon of light.

Syntax is seen in all sacred text
dopamine dances
just out of frame.

They threw the holy water out
with The Baphomet
when they deemed heretical
the deep knowledge of the womb.

They drowned the babies
in the bath water
in writing Ephesians 5:22

There lies the star of David,
Propped up against the sultry pentacles
Sharp edges for round corners.
Round with,
or without his permission.

They dislodged the wheels
to win the contest!

of who can spin into oblivion—
The fastest.
The bestest.
With the most soldiers.

Some don't partake in the spectacle

Some of us slide fingers
behind curtains—
The silk that separates
The Saved ones from the *Damned ones.*
The Lost ones from the *Found ones*

Mother, forgive us
we have not sinned enough.

Atoms french kiss every day
as if touch were not
invented by algebra

Mother hear our prayer

You Are Loved (Just the Same)

Yes, nightshade,
some things grow faster in the dark
Jerusalem cherry,
You and I.

Yes, life can crush
all 206 bones in your body—
and leave you kneeling
thanking cracked menisci—
for being yours to break.

Love will resurrect you stronger,
whether you pray
or don't.
It will comfort you,
whether you believe it will,
or won't.

No matter if you pray—
or scream to the river
at traffic lights
sob into pillows—

love is not reserved
for those who claim to know
its one true source

As if
the long-credited bringer of change
were not subject

to it's name

I believe,
there is a special place in Jesus' heart
for the lamb whose cries
sound like sailors with scurvy
stubbing necrotic toes
after a night of rum.

I believe,
He puts the 'broken' ones
The 'lost' ones
in the same rank
as the bowed heads
every Sunday

Between you and me,
Belladonna,
I think he loves us a bit more

No matter your zip code
or to which God you pray,
You are loved, belladonna.
You Are Loved
(Just the Same.)

Acknowledgements

To my friends—thank you for helping me find my way back to a version of myself I didn't know was missing. You listened, encouraged, and reminded me what I was capable of. You let me bounce ideas, take detours, rewrite lines, and weight the risks of choosing a life that feels like freedom.
Hannah and Tricia, thank you for encouraging me to quit the job that was never in alignment with my calling. You saw the spark before I did.

To my sister, Michelle, and my mother, Christine— thank you for not having heart attacks when I told you I quit my job to pursue writing full time. Your grace and confidence gave me courage.

To my powerful illustrator, Briana Yarrington, thank you for the visual magic you lent this book—few could capture the polarities these poems grapple with, but you did.

To the writers whose work clung to me like static—I couldn't get your words off of me without writing something through them. This book is built on your shoulders. Writers including, but not limited to: Sylvia Plath, Robert Frost, Walt Whitman, Kim Addonizio, Nicholas Sparks, George R. R. Martin, Chelsie Diane, Ernest Hemingway, Adam Smith, Theodor Seuss Geisel, F. Scott Fitzgerald, O. Henry, Emily Brontë, George Orwell and William Butler Yeats.

To the self-selected professors I studied under at YouTube University:
Dr. Stephen Cheeke, Dr. Octavia Cox, and tim mcgee.

(name is purposefully lowercased since that's how it appears on his YouTube channel— I love it and it's in keeping with the scrappy nature of this book.) If you, too, are a bold swimmer, you might wade into tim's work at *learnstrong.net*. Thank you, tim, for making the dives deeper.

To Tony DeSare, an incredible musician and songwriter friend— thank you for letting me borrow your trained eyes and ears as one of the first to see my writing. Your support, insight, and belief in my voice helped bring this book to life. Recognition from someone who consistently puts beauty into the world makes it easier to believe it could come from oneself, too.

To my poetry teacher, Chelsie Diane—thank you for helping me find my flame and guarding it like treasure.

Lastly, to anyone who presented me with thorns—
It'd be rude not to mention you.
Thank you for the roses.
The dragons like them too.

— *Lauren Kalli*

www.ingramcontent.com/pod-product-compliance
Lightning Source LLC
Chambersburg PA
CBHW020419150626
46554CB00014B/2152